How quick come the reasons
for approving what we like.

JANE AUSTEN

*Don't indulge your ego
at the expense of your soul.*

THE MESSAGE

LITERARY PORTALS TO PRAYER™

JANE AUSTEN

ILLUMINATED BY

COMPILED AND INTRODUCED BY

RACHEL HART WINTER

JANE AUSTEN
Illuminated by The Message
Compiled and introduced by Rachel Hart Winter

Series Editor, Gregory F. Augustine Pierce
Design and typesetting by Harvest Graphics
Cover image under license from Bigstock

Published by ACTA Publications, 4848 N. Clark St.,
Chicago, IL 60640, (800) 397-2282, actapublications.com

Library of Congress Number: 2017950184
ISBN: 978-0-87946-625-1
Printed in the United States of America by Total Printing Systems
Year 30 29 28 27 26 25 24 23 22 21 20 19 18 17
Printing 12 11 10 9 8 7 6 5 4 3 2 First

✪ Text printed on 30% post-consumer recycled paper

CONTENTS

A NOTE FROM THE PUBLISHER / 9

INTRODUCTION / 11

SOURCES / 15

PORTALS TO PRAYER / 16

SCRIPTURE INDEX / 117

ABOUT RACHEL HART WINTER / 119

Prayer is sometimes difficult. Perhaps we need spiritual inspiration. Something to reignite our spiritual life. A way to initiate a new and fruitful spiritual direction.

Great literature can do these things: inspire, ignite, and initiate.

Which is why ACTA Publications is publishing a series of "Literary Portals to Prayer." The idea is simple: take insightful passages from great authors whose work has stood the test of time and illuminate each selection with a well-chosen quotation from the Bible on the same theme.

To do this, we use a relatively new translation by Eugene Peterson called *The Message: Catholic/Ecumenical Edition*. It is a fresh, compelling, challenging, and faith-filled translation of the Scriptures from ancient languages into contemporary American English that sounds as if it was written yesterday. *The Message* may be new to you, or you may already know it well, but see if it doesn't illuminate these writings of Jane Austen in delightful ways.

We publish the books in this series in a size that can easily fit in pocket or purse and find a spot on kitchen table, bed stand, work bench, study desk, or exercise machine. These books are meant to be used in a variety of ways. And we feature a variety of authors so you can find the one or ones that can kick-start your prayer life.

So enjoy these portals to prayer by Jane Austen illuminated by *The Message*. And look for others in this series, including Louisa May Alcott, Hans Christian Andersen, Charles Dickens, Elizabeth Gaskell, Herman Melville, William Shakespeare, Edith Wharton, Walt Whitman, and others. Consider them, if you will, literary *lectio divina*.

Gregory F. Augustine Pierce
President and Publisher
ACTA Publications

REGARDING SPELLING, PUNCTUATION, AND CAPITALIZATION IN AUSTEN'S WORK

In very few instances, we have changed British spellings of words to American versions. Punctuation and capitalization we have left alone, unless it might confuse the modern reader. Where we start a quote in mid-sentence or add a word for clarity, we merely do so, rather than distract the reader with ellipses or brackets. First names have been inserted where a pronoun needs clarification.

I have always believed that reading literature is much like prayer. Words on the written page have the ability to cause me to shout for joy, sadness, excitement, despair—all of the things we often share with God in our prayers and hold in the deepest places of our heart and soul. Somehow when a talented author like Jane Austen says things so eloquently and prophetically that it captures exactly what we are feeling, it seems only right to sing out in gratitude that we are not alone on this journey in life, that perhaps some of the things we are experiencing are as timeless as the biblical authors referred to in their day.

Austen speaks to the truth of her time in a way that is a lesson for all of us. There is a reason many of us remember our first time reading Austen. She helped us see and understand the world, and as a result we become better able to know ourselves and God. She pays deep attention to the ordinary details of our lives. As many theologians, wise scholars, and authors remind us, it is in these ordinary, everyday moments that we are often invited into the presence of God. Austen reminds us that one of the gifts of any life, but certainly the spiritual life, is the ability to notice the people, places, and beauty around us.

Biblical authors, excellent literary figures, and poets over the ages share in common the need to pay attention to the details of the world around us. Slowing down enough to observe, exhibiting enough courage, taking time to express our love, and offering deep gratitude to our God—these are the things that seem to underpin a life well lived. Austen lived courageously, writing in a time when women were not a part of the literary community. She lived authentically, knowing her talent and sharing it in books, in prayers, and in a vast collection of letters. She lived faithfully, sharing with all of us over the centuries her celebration of words. More than ever today we need attentive descriptions of faith to find meaning in our lives. Austen can be our guide, and we are lucky to be the recipients of her wit and wisdom.

In re-reading Jane Austen over the past few months in preparation for this book, I encountered a favorite author from my youth at a new moment in my life. I am now a mother of three. Austen's care for and love of family are found throughout her writings. It is that devotion to family that impacts me most at present. She was extremely close to her family, her siblings, her nieces, her parents. She was a woman with a strong faith, surrounded by people of faith as the daughter of an Anglican minister and herself the author of profound prayers. Her passion for literary art mirrored her love of humanity and the world around her. She used her pen and paper to share that love with the world, and centuries later we are still recipients of her love and grace.

Austen "cared a great deal about accuracy" and wanted her novels to be "true to life." For this reason she has been compared to Charles Darwin—albeit his skill was as a naturalist and hers as a novelist. Author Peter Graham describes both as "keen observers of the world before them, who excelled in noticing microscopic particulars and in understanding the cosmic significance of those small details." It is Austen's ability to penetrate the ordinary encounters of life and to describe them in a way that offers new meaning that invite us to find our own meaning again and again in her novels.

Austen cuts to the heart of the human condition, revealing our deepest sense of who we are, the relationships we value, and even the natural world we occupy. It is her acute sense of the real that she conveys on the page—for example, describing a strawberry in a way that invites readers to consider again the simple pleasures in life. Her ability to describe the emotions we all experience as humans—from love and longing to sadness and lament—and her precision and clarity of expression allow us to relate in new ways to the world and to one another.

Austen offers one of the best depictions of the human person recorded in literature. The beautiful way she reveals for us character development—her sense of love and commitment, her ability to share the experience of loss and longing—all of these lend themselves to her incredible perspective on both the wisdom and wit of the human community.

Join me, then, as we explore some of her most profound passages alongside the equally compelling and relevant translation of the Bible—*The Message* by Eugene Peterson. *The Message* is appropriate as an "illumination" of literature because it speaks to us in a language accessible for people today, in the same way that Jane Austen has spoken to generations of readers across the last two centuries.

Rachel Hart Winter
Dominican University
River Forest, Illinois

JANE AUSTEN

SELECTIONS FROM

Sense and Sensibility, 1811
Pride and Prejudice, 1813
Mansfield Park, 1814
Emma, 1815
Northanger Abbey, 1818*
Persuasion, 1818*
Minor Works, 1818*

*published posthumously

VARIOUS WAYS

Elinor, this eldest daughter whose advice was so effectual, possessed a strength of understanding, and coolness of judgment, which qualified her, though only nineteen, to be the counsellor of her mother, and enabled her frequently to counteract, to the advantage of them all, that eagerness of mind in Mrs. Dashwood which must generally have led to imprudence. She had an excellent heart; her disposition was affectionate, and her feelings were strong: but she knew how to govern them: it was a knowledge which her mother had yet to learn, and which one of her sisters had resolved never to be taught. Marianne's abilities were, in many respects, quite equal to Elinor's. She was sensible and clever; but eager in everything; her sorrows, her joys, could have no moderation.

SENSE AND SENSIBILITY, CHAPTER I

VARIOUS WAYS

What I want to talk about now is the various ways God's Spirit gets worked into our lives. This is complex and often misunderstood, but I want you to be informed and knowledgeable....

God's various gifts are handed out everywhere; but they all originate in God's Spirit. God's various ministries are carried out everywhere; but they all originate in God's Spirit. God's various expressions of power are in action everywhere; but God himself is behind it all. Each person is given something to do that shows who God is: Everyone gets in on it, everyone benefits. All kinds of things are handed out by the Spirit, and to all kinds of people!

The variety is wonderful: wise counsel, clear understanding, simple trust, healing the sick, miraculous acts, proclamation, distinguishing between spirits, tongues, interpretation of tongues. All these gifts have a common origin, but are handed out one by one by the one Spirit of God. He decides who gets what, and when.

I CORINTHIANS I, 4-11

ULTIMATE HONEY AND SWEET MILK

A continuance in a place where everything reminded her of former delight, was exactly what suited her mind. In seasons of cheerfulness, no temper could be more cheerful than hers, or possess, in a greater degree, that sanguine expectation of happiness which is happiness itself. But in sorrow she must be equally carried away by her fancy, and as far beyond consolation as in pleasure she was beyond alloy.

SENSE AND SENSIBILITY, CHAPTER 2

ULTIMATE HONEY AND SWEET MILK

It's fanfares, ruffles and flourishes—hail to Lady Wisdom! God echoes her praises, and so do all the people. The presence of the Most High she's well acquainted with, in plain view of God she conducts herself nicely. In the assembly of the most low, she feels most at home: in the holy places she's well-received. In the company of the elect, she's welcome: among the blessed she's a role model.

Lady Wisdom has to say....

"Come over here to me, one and all, who can't wait to see me. Have I got something for you! I've got bushels and bushels from my garden. My teaching is ultimate honey; my heritage is sweet milk. Who eats me satisfies a hunger; who drinks me quenches a thirst; who hears me fulfills a longing; who works with me won't commit a sin; who makes sense out of me will have eternal life."

SIRACH 24:1-4, 26-31

SET THE HILLS TO DANCING

The whole country about them abounded in beautiful walks. The high downs which invited them from almost every window of the cottage to seek the exquisite enjoyment of air on their summits, were a happy alternative when the dirt of the valleys beneath shut up their superior beauties; and towards one of these hills did Marianne and Margaret one memorable morning direct their steps, attracted by the partial sunshine of a showery sky, and unable longer to bear the confinement which the settled rain of the two preceding days had occasioned.

SENSE AND SENSIBILITY, CHAPTER 9

SET THE HILLS TO DANCING

Oh, visit the earth,
ask her to join the dance!
Deck her out in spring showers,
fill the God-River with living water.
Paint the wheat fields golden.
Creation was made for this!
Drench the plowed fields,
soak the dirt clods
With rainfall as harrow and rake
bring her to blossom and fruit.
Snow-crown the peaks with splendor,
scatter rose petals down your paths,
All through the wild meadows, rose petals.
Set the hills to dancing.

PSALM 65:9-12

STAY THE COURSE

Marianne was awake the whole night, and she wept the greatest part of it. She got up with a headache, was unable to talk, and unwilling to take any nourishment; giving pain every moment to her mother and sisters, and forbidding all attempt at consolation from either. Her sensibility was potent enough!

When breakfast was over, she walked out by herself, and wandered about the village of Allenham, indulging the recollection of past enjoyment and crying over the present reverse for the chief of the morning.

SENSE AND SENSIBILITY, CHAPTER 16

STAY THE COURSE

You're blessed when you stay on course,
*   walking steadily on the road revealed by* GOD.
You're blessed when you follow his directions,
*   doing your best to find him.*
That's right—you don't go off on your own;
*   you walk straight along the road he set.*
You, GOD, *prescribed the right way to live;*
*   now you expect us to live it.*
Oh, that my steps might be steady,
*   keeping to the course you set;*
Then I'd never have any regrets
*   in comparing my life with your counsel.*
I thank you for speaking straight from your heart;
*   I learn the pattern of your righteous ways.*
I'm going to do what you tell me to do;
*   don't ever walk off and leave me.*

PSALM 119:1-9

SQUINTING IN A FOG

"Come, come; this is all an effusion of immediate want of spirits, Edward. You are in a melancholy humor, and fancy that anyone unlike yourself must be happy. But remember that the pain of parting from friends will be felt by everybody at times, whatever be their education or state. Know your own happiness. You want nothing but patience—or give it a more fascinating name, call it hope."

SENSE AND SENSIBILITY, CHAPTER 19

SQUINTING IN A FOG

We don't yet see things clearly. We're squinting in a fog, peering through a mist. But it won't be long before the weather clears and the sun shines bright! We'll see it all then, see it all as clearly as God sees us, knowing him directly just as he knows us!

But for right now, until that completeness, we have three things to do to lead us toward that consummation: Trust steadily in God, hope unswervingly, love extravagantly. And the best of the three is love.

I CORINTHIANS 13:12-13

TASTE AND SAVOR HIS DELICIOUS LOVE

Marianne paused, and added in a lower voice, "If I could but know *his* heart, everything would become easy."

Elinor, who had now been for some time reflecting on the propriety or impropriety of speedily hazarding her narration, without feeling at all nearer decision than at first, heard this; and perceiving that as reflection did nothing, resolution must do all, soon found herself leading to the fact....

A thousand inquiries sprung up from her heart, but she dared not urge one. She caught every syllable with panting eagerness; her hand, unknowingly to herself, closely pressed her sister's, and tears covered her cheeks.

SENSE AND SENSIBILITY, CHAPTER 46

TASTE AND SAVOR HIS DELICIOUS LOVE

As an apricot tree stands out in the forest,
    my lover stands above the young men in town.
All I want is to sit in his shade,
    to taste and savor his delicious love.
He took me home with him for a festive meal,
    but his eyes feasted on me!

Oh! Give me something refreshing to eat—and quickly!
    Apricots, raisins—anything.
    I'm about to faint with love!
His left hand cradles my head,
    and his right arm encircles my waist!

Oh, let me warn you, sisters in Jerusalem,
    by the gazelles, yes, by all the wild deer:
Don't excite love, don't stir it up,
    until the time is ripe—and you're ready.

SONGS OF SONGS 2:3-7

BORN FROM ABOVE

"Oh! you are a great deal too apt, you know, to like people in general. You never see a fault in anybody. All the world are good and agreeable in your eyes. I never heard you speak ill of a human being in my life."

"I would wish not to be hasty in censuring any one; but I always speak what I think."

"I know you do; and it is *that* which makes the wonder. With *your* good sense to be so honestly blind to the follies and nonsense of others! Affectation of candour is common enough;—one meets it everywhere. But to be candid without ostentation or design—to take the good of everybody's character and make it still better, and say nothing of the bad—belongs to you alone."

PRIDE AND PREJUDICE, CHAPTER 4

BORN FROM ABOVE

Jesus said, "You're not listening. Let me say it again. Unless a person submits to this original creation—the 'wind-hovering-over-the-water' creation, the invisible moving the visible, a baptism into a new life—it's not possible to enter God's kingdom. When you look at a baby, it's just that: a body you can look at and touch. But the person who takes shape within is formed by something you can't see and touch—the Spirit— and becomes a living spirit.

"So don't be so surprised when I tell you that you have to be 'born from above'—out of this world, so to speak. You know well enough how the wind blows this way and that. You hear it rustling through the trees, but you have no idea where it comes from or where it's headed next. That's the way it is with everyone 'born from above' by the wind of God, the Spirit of God."

JOHN 3:5-8

NOTHING BUT SMOKE

"Pride," observed Mary, who piqued herself upon the solidity of her reflections, "is a very common failing, I believe. By all that I have ever read, I am convinced that it is very common indeed; that human nature is particularly prone to it, and that there are very few of us who do not cherish a feeling of self-complacency on the score of some quality or other, real or imaginary. Vanity and pride are different things, though the words are often used synonymously. A person may be proud without being vain. Pride relates more to our opinion of ourselves, vanity to what we would have others think of us."

PRIDE AND PREJUDICE, CHAPTER 5

NOTHING BUT SMOKE

Smoke, nothing but smoke. [That's what the Quester says.]
  There's nothing to anything—it's all smoke.
What's there to show for a lifetime of work,
  a lifetime of working your fingers to the bone?
One generation goes its way, the next one arrives,
  but nothing changes—it's business as usual
    for old planet earth.
The sun comes up and the sun goes down,
  then does it again, and again—the same old round.
The wind blows south, the wind blows north.
  Around and around and around it blows,
  blowing this way, then that—the whirling, erratic wind.

ECCLESIASTES 1:2-6

AND SPITTING INTO THE WIND

"The country," said Darcy, "can in general supply but few subjects for such a study. In a country neighborhood you move in a very confined and unvarying society."

"But people themselves alter so much, that there is something new to be observed in them for ever."

"Yes, indeed," cried Mrs. Bennet, offended by his manner of mentioning a country neighborhood. "I assure you there is quite as much of that going on in the country as in town."

PRIDE AND PREJUDICE, CHAPTER 9

AND SPITTING INTO THE WIND

Call me "the Quester." I've been king over Israel in Jerusalem. I looked most carefully into everything, searched out all that is done on this earth. And let me tell you, there's not much to write home about. God hasn't made it easy for us. I've seen it all and it's nothing but smoke—smoke, and spitting into the wind.

> *Life's a corkscrew that can't be straightened,*
> *A minus that won't add up.*

I said to myself, "I know more and I'm wiser than anyone before me in Jerusalem. I've stockpiled wisdom and knowledge." What I've finally concluded is that so-called wisdom and knowledge are mindless and witless—nothing but spitting into the wind.

> *Much learning earns you much trouble.*
> *The more you know, the more you hurt.*

ECCLESIASTES 1:12-18

MY DEAR LOST LOVE

"And so ended his affection," said Elizabeth impatiently. "There has been many a one, I fancy, overcome in the same way. I wonder who first discovered the efficacy of poetry in driving away love!"

"I have been used to consider poetry as the *food* of love," said Darcy.

"Of a fine, stout, healthy love it may. Everything nourishes what is strong already.

PRIDE AND PREJUDICE, CHAPTER 9

MY DEAR LOST LOVE

Restless in bed and sleepless through the night,
  I longed for my lover.
  I wanted him desperately. His absence was painful.
So I got up, went out and roved the city,
  hunting through streets and down alleys.
I wanted my lover in the worst way!
  I looked high and low, and didn't find him.
And then the night watchmen found me
  as they patrolled the darkened city.
  "Have you seen my dear lost love?" I asked.
No sooner had I left them than I found him,
  found my dear lost love.
I threw my arms around him and held him tight,
  wouldn't let him go until I had him home again,
  safe at home beside the fire

SONG OF SONGS 3:3-4

MANY GREAT THINGS

"I declare after all there is no enjoyment like reading! How much sooner one tires of anything than of a book!—When I have a house of my own, I shall be miserable if I have not an excellent library."

PRIDE AND PREJUDICE, CHAPTER 11

MANY GREAT THINGS

Many great things have come down through God's words and teachings of the prophets and in the commentaries on them. For the doctrine and wisdom contained therein, we have the house of Israel to thank and praise.

Those who read and understand such writings have studied the subject matter and, to a great extent, have mastered it. Those of us for whom the matter was beyond our comprehension have depended on scholars to simplify and break it down for us.

My grandfather was one of the great popularizers. He devoted a good part of his life to pouring over the sacred texts. He would never say he'd mastered the material, but he did feel that he's acquired a certain proficiency. Is it a wonder then that he wanted to add a bit of his own wisdom—this book—to the growing literature, something to help teachers teach and followers of the wisdom live the sort of life described in God's word?

…I burned many a new candle working day and night on the project—translating, editing, writing, and publishing the work myself. All the while I kept in the middle the audience who would appreciate the work: those who wished to school themselves in the customs and the practices of the Israelites and live the life of God's word as in Jerusalem.

SIRACH I (PROLOGUE)

37

DO YOU KNOW THE WAY?

"My dear, dear aunt," Elizabeth rapturously cried, "what delight! what felicity! You give me fresh life and vigor. Adieu to disappointment and spleen. What are men to rocks and mountains? Oh! what hours of transport we shall spend! And when we *do* return, it shall not be like other travellers, without being able to give one accurate idea of anything. We *will* know where we have gone—we *will* recollect what we have seen. Lakes, mountains, and rivers shall not be jumbled together in our imaginations; nor, when we attempt to describe any particular scene, will we begin quarrelling about its relative situation."

PRIDE AND PREJUDICE, CHAPTER 27

DO YOU KNOW THE WAY?

Toby went out to find a bodyguard, though he didn't know how to choose honest from dishonest. In the first few minutes, however, he bumped into a fellow lounging about; he was certainly large and strong enough for the job, but there was something in his eyes that was unsettling.

"Where do you hail from," asked Toby.

"From the children of Israel, your kind of people, and I'm looking for work," the man replied.

"Do you know the way to Media?"

"Been there many times, staying with a relative of mine, who lives in Rages. Let's see. From Ecbatana to Rages—that's a trip from the plains to the mountains."

"Hold on, sir. I have to go in and consult with my father. But you're just the sort of person we're looking for, and we'll pay the going rate."

"Okay, but I don't have all day."

Toby told his father about the muscular fellow outside. "He's one of us, the children of Israel. He said he'd go with me."

TOBIT 5:4-9

LET'S PRACTICE REAL LOVE

"In vain have I struggled. It will not do. My feelings will not be repressed. You must allow me to tell you how ardently I admire and love you."

PRIDE AND PREJUDICE CHAPTER 34

LET'S PRACTICE REAL LOVE

My dear children, let's not just talk about love; let's practice real love. This is the only way we'll know we're living truly, living in God's reality. It's also the way to shut down debilitating self-criticism, even when there is something to it. For God is greater than our worried hearts and knows more about us than we do ourselves.

I JOHN 3:18-20

NO LONGER CONDEMNING OURSELVES

"How despicably have I acted!" Elizabeth cried; "I, who have prided myself on my discernment! I, who have valued myself on my abilities! who have often disdained the generous candour of my sister, and gratified my vanity in useless or blameable distrust. How humiliating is this discovery! yet, how just a humiliation! Had I been in love, I could not have been more wretchedly blind. But vanity, not love, has been my folly. Pleased with the preference of one, and offended by the neglect of the other, on the very beginning of our acquaintance, I have courted prepossession and ignorance, and driven reason away, where either were concerned. Till this moment I never knew myself."

PRIDE AND PREJUDICE, CHAPTER 36

NO LONGER CONDEMNING OURSELVES

And friends, once that's taken care of and we're no longer accusing or condemning ourselves, we're bold and free before God! We're able to stretch our hands out and receive what we asked for because we're doing what he said, doing what pleases him. Again, this is God's command: to believe in his personally named Son, Jesus Christ. He told us to love each other, in line with the original command. As we keep his commands, we live deeply and surely in him, and he lives in us. And this is how we experience his deep and abiding presence in us: by the Spirit he gave us.

I JOHN 3:21-24

FROM THE VERY FIRST DAY

Elizabeth's spirits soon rising to playfulness again, she wanted Mr. Darcy to account for his having ever fallen in love with her. "How could you begin?" said she. "I can comprehend your going on charmingly, when you had once made a beginning; but what could set you off in the first place?"

"I cannot fix on the hour, or the spot, or the look, or the words, which laid the foundation. It is too long ago. I was in the middle before I knew that I *had* begun."

PRIDE AND PREJUDICE, CHAPTER 60

FROM THE VERY FIRST DAY

From the very first day, we were there, taking it all in—we heard it with our own ears, saw it with our own eyes, verified it with our own hands. The Word of Life appeared right before our eyes; we saw it happen! And now we're telling you in most sober prose that what we witnessed was, incredibly, this: The infinite Life of God himself took shape before us.

We saw it, we heard it, and now we're telling you so you can experience it along with us, this experience of communion with the Father and his Son, Jesus Christ. Our motive for writing is simply this: We want you to enjoy this, too. Your joy will double our joy!

I JOHN I:I-4

BUY EDUCATION

"Give a girl an education and introduce her properly into the world, and ten to one but she has the means of settling well, without further expense to anybody."

MANSFIELD PARK, CHAPTER I

BUY EDUCATION

Listen with respect to the father who raised you,
 and when your mother grows old, don't neglect her.
Buy truth—don't sell it for love or money;
 buy wisdom, buy education, buy insight.
Parents rejoice when their children turn out well;
 wise children become proud parents.
So make your father happy!
 Make your mother proud!

PROVERBS 23:22-25

REKINDLING BURNED-OUT LIVES

"I thoroughly understand you," cried Mrs. Norris, "you are everything that is generous and considerate, and I am sure we shall never disagree on this point. Whatever I can do, as you well know, I am always ready enough to do for the good of those I love; and, though I could never feel for this little girl the hundredth part of the regard I bear your own dear children, nor consider her, in any respect, so much my own, I should hate myself if I were capable of neglecting her. Is not she a sister's child? and could I bear to see her want while I had a bit of bread to give her?"

MANSFIELD PARK, CHAPTER I

REKINDLING BURNED-OUT LIVES

God brings death and God brings life,
brings down to the grave and raises up.
God brings poverty and God brings wealth;
he lowers, he also lifts up.
He puts poor people on their feet again;
he rekindles burned-out lives with fresh hope,
Restoring dignity and respect to their lives—
a place in the sun!
For the very structures of earth are God's;
he has laid out his operations on a firm foundation.

I SAMUEL 2:6-8

FEARLESS NO MATTER WHAT

"I know so many who have married in the full expectation and confidence of some one particular advantage in the connection, or accomplishment, or good quality in the person, who have found themselves entirely deceived, and been obliged to put up with exactly the reverse. What is this but a take in?"

"My dear child, there must be a little imagination here. I beg your pardon, but I cannot quite believe you. Depend upon it, you see but half. You see the evil, but you do not see the consolation. There will be little rubs and disappointments everywhere, and we are all apt to expect too much; but then, if one scheme of happiness fails, human nature turns to another; if the first calculation is wrong, we make a second better: we find comfort somewhere—and those evil-minded observers, dearest Mary, who make much of a little, are more taken in and deceived than the parties themselves."

MANSFIELD PARK, CHAPTER 5

FEARLESS NO MATTER WHAT

Stay on good terms with each other, held together by love. Be ready with a meal or a bed when it's needed. Why, some have extended hospitality to angels without ever knowing it! Regard prisoners as if you were in prison with them. Look on victims of abuse as if what happened to them had happened to you. Honor marriage, and guard the sacredness of sexual intimacy between wife and husband. God draws a firm line against casual and illicit sex.

Don't be obsessed with getting more material things. Be relaxed with what you have. Since God assured us, "I'll never let you down, never walk off and leave you," we can boldly quote,

> *God is there, ready to help;*
> *I'm fearless no matter what.*
> *Who or what can get to me?*

HEBREWS 13:1-6

QUIETLY AND UNOBTRUSIVELY

Their road was through a pleasant country; and Fanny, whose rides had never been extensive, was soon beyond her knowledge, and was very happy in observing all that was new, and admiring all that was pretty. She was not often invited to join in the conversation of the others, nor did she desire it. Her own thoughts and reflections were habitually her best companions; and, in observing the appearance of the country, the bearings of the roads, the difference of soil, the state of the harvest, the cottages, the cattle, the children, she found entertainment that could only have been heightened by having Edmund to speak to of what she felt.

MANSFIELD PARK, CHAPTER 8

QUIETLY AND UNOBTRUSIVELY

Jesus said, "You've seen them in action, I'm sure—'playactors' I call them—treating prayer meeting and street corner alike as a stage, acting compassionate as long as someone is watching, playing to the crowds. They get applause, true, but that's all they get. When you help someone out, don't think about how it looks. Just do it—quietly and unobtrusively. That is the way your God, who conceived you in love, working behind the scenes, helps you out.

"And when you come before God, don't turn that into a theatrical production either. All these people making a regular show out of their prayers, hoping for stardom! Do you think God sits in a box seat?

"Here's what I want you to do: Find a quiet, secluded place so you won't be tempted to role-play before God. Just be there as simply and honestly as you can manage. The focus will shift from you to God, and you will begin to sense his grace."

MATTHEW 6:2-6

DON'T FOOL YOURSELF

A fine preacher is followed and admired; but it is not in fine preaching only that a good clergyman will be useful in his parish and his neighborhood, where the parish and neighborhood are of a size capable of knowing his private character and observing his general conduct, which in London can rarely be the case.

MANSFIELD PARK, CHAPTER 9

DON'T FOOL YOURSELF

Don't fool yourself into thinking that you are a listener when you are anything but, letting the Word go in one ear and out the other. Act on what you hear! Those who hear and don't act are like those who glance in the mirror, walk away, and two minutes later have no idea who they are, what they look like.

But whoever catches a glimpse of the revealed counsel of God—the free life!—even out of the corner of his or her eye, and sticks with it, is no distracted scatterbrain but a man or woman of action. That person will find delight and affirmation in the action.

Anyone who sets himself or herself up as "religious" by talking a good game is self-deceived. This kind of religion is hot air and only hot air. Real religion, the kind that passes muster before God the Father, is this: Reach out to the homeless and loveless in their plight, and guard against corruption from the godless world.

JAMES 1:22-27

LET ME CATCH MY BREATH

"I shall soon be rested," said Fanny; "to sit in the shade on a fine day, and look upon verdure, is the most perfect refreshment."

MANSFIELD PARK, CHAPTER 9

LET ME CATCH MY BREATH

God, *my shepherd!*
   I don't need a thing.
You have bedded me down in lush meadows,
   you find me quiet pools to drink from.
True to your word,
   you let me catch my breath
   and send me in the right direction.

Even when the way goes through
   Death Valley,
I'm not afraid
   when you walk at my side.
Your trusty shepherd's crook
   makes me feel secure.

PSALM 23:1-4

EVERYTHING NEW

"Here's harmony!" said Fanny; "here's repose! Here's what may leave all painting and all music behind, and what poetry only can attempt to describe! Here's what may tranquillise every care, and lift the heart to rapture! When I look out on such a night as this, I feel as if there could be neither wickedness nor sorrow in the world; and there certainly would be less of both if the sublimity of Nature were more attended to, and people were carried more out of themselves by contemplating such a scene."

MANSFIELD PARK, CHAPTER 11

EVERYTHING NEW

I heard a voice thunder from the Throne:
"Look! Look!
God has moved into the neighborhood,
making his home with men and women!
They're his people, he's their God.
He'll wipe every tear from their eyes.
Death is gone for good
—tears gone, crying gone, pain gone—
all the first order of things gone."

The Enthroned continued,
"Look!
I'm making everything new.
Write it all down—
each word dependable and accurate."

REVELATION 21:3-5

NEVER FORGET

"How wonderful, how very wonderful the operations of time, and the changes of the human mind!" And following the latter train of thought, Fanny soon afterwards added: "If any one faculty of our nature may be called more wonderful than the rest, I do think it is memory. There seems something more speakingly incomprehensible in the powers, the failures, the inequalities of memory, than in any other of our intelligences. The memory is sometimes so retentive, so serviceable, so obedient; at others, so bewildered and so weak; and at others again, so tyrannic, so beyond control! We are, to be sure, a miracle every way; but our powers of recollecting and of forgetting do seem peculiarly past finding out."

MANSFIELD PARK, CHAPTER 22

NEVER FORGET

Every time I think of you—and I think of you often!—I thank God for your lives of free and open access to God, given by Jesus. There's no end to what has happened in you—it's beyond speech, beyond knowledge. The evidence of Christ has been clearly verified in your lives.

Just think—you don't need a thing, you've got it all! All God's gifts are right in front of you as you wait expectantly for our Master Jesus to arrive on the scene for the Finale. And not only that, but God himself is right alongside to keep you steady and on track until things are all wrapped up by Jesus. God, who got you started in this spiritual adventure, shares with us the life of his Son and our Master Jesus. He will never give up on you. Never forget that.

I CORINTHIANS I:4-9

IT MIGHT BE GOOD THEATER

"It is as a dream, a pleasant dream!" Crawford exclaimed, breaking forth again, after a few minutes' musing. "I shall always look back on our theatricals with exquisite pleasure. There was such an interest, such an animation, such a spirit diffused. Everybody felt it. We were all alive. There was employment, hope, solicitude, bustle, for every hour of the day. Always some little objection, some little doubt, some little anxiety to be got over. I never was happier."

MANSFIELD PARK, CHAPTER 23

IT MIGHT BE GOOD THEATER

Jesus said:
"Be especially careful when you are trying to be good
so that you don't make a performance out of it.
It might be good theater,
but the God who made you won't be applauding....
Give your entire attention to what God is doing right now,
and don't get worked up about what may
or may not happen tomorrow.
God will help you deal with whatever hard things come up
when the time comes."

MATTHEW 6:1, 34

THE INTEGRITY OF YOUR TEACHERS

"A sermon, well delivered, is more uncommon even than prayers well read. A sermon, good in itself, is no rare thing. It is more difficult to speak well than to compose well; that is, the rules and trick of composition are oftener an object of study. A thoroughly good sermon, thoroughly well delivered, is a capital gratification. I can never hear such a one without the greatest admiration and respect, and more than half a mind to take orders and preach myself. There is something in the eloquence of the pulpit, when it is really eloquence, which is entitled to the highest praise and honor. The preacher who can touch and affect such an heterogeneous mass of hearers, on subjects limited, and long worn threadbare in all common hands; who can say anything new or striking, anything that rouses the attention without offending the taste, or wearing out the feelings of his hearers, is a man whom one could not, in his public capacity, honour enough."

MANSFIELD PARK, CHAPTER 34

THE INTEGRITY OF YOUR TEACHERS

You've been a good apprentice to me, a part of my teaching, my manner of life, direction, faith, steadiness, love, patience, troubles, sufferings—suffering along with me in all the grief I had to put up with…. And you also well know that God rescued me! Anyone who wants to live all out for Christ is in for a lot of trouble; there's no getting around it. Unscrupulous con men will continue to exploit the faith. They're as deceived as the people they lead astray. As long as they are out there, things can only get worse.

But don't let it faze you. Stick with what you learned and believed, sure of the integrity of your teachers—why, you took in the sacred Scriptures with your mother's milk! There's nothing like the written Word of God for showing you the way to salvation through faith in Christ Jesus. Every part of Scripture is God-breathed and useful one way or another—showing us truth, exposing our rebellion, correcting our mistakes, training us to live God's way. Through the Word we are put together and shaped up for the tasks God has for us.

2 TIMOTHY 3:10-17

THE TUNE I DANCE TO

Let other pens dwell on guilt and misery. I quit such odious subjects as soon as I can, impatient to restore everybody, not greatly in fault themselves, to tolerable comfort, and to have done with all the rest.

MANSFIELD PARK, CHAPTER 48

THE TUNE I DANCE TO

Now comfort me so I can live, really live;
  your revelation is the tune I dance to.
Let the fast-talking tricksters be exposed as frauds;
  they tried to sell me a bill of goods,
  but I kept my mind fixed on your counsel.
Let those who fear you turn to me
  for evidence of your wise guidance.
And let me live whole and holy, soul and body,
  so I can always walk with my head held high.

PSALM 119:76-80

I RELISH EVERYTHING

Emma was so busy in admiring those soft blue eyes, in talking and listening, and forming all these schemes in the in-betweens, that the evening flew away at a very unusual rate; and the supper-table, which always closed such parties, and for which she had been used to sit and watch the due time, was all set out and ready, and moved forwards to the fire, before she was aware. With an alacrity beyond the common impulse of a spirit which yet was never indifferent to the credit of doing everything well and attentively, with the real good-will of a mind delighted with its own ideas, did she then do all the honors of the meal, and help and recommend the minced chicken and scalloped oysters with an urgency which she knew would be acceptable to the early hours and civil scruples of their guests.

EMMA, CHAPTER 3

I RELISH EVERYTHING

How can a young person live a clean life?
   By carefully reading the map of your Word.
I'm single-minded in pursuit of you;
   don't let me miss the road signs you've posted.
I've banked your promises in the vault of my heart
   so I won't sin myself bankrupt.
Be blessed, GOD;
   train me in your ways of wise living.
I'll transfer to my lips
   all the counsel that comes from your mouth;
I delight far more in what you tell me about living
   than in gathering a pile of riches.
I ponder every morsel of wisdom from you,
   I attentively watch how you've done it.
I relish everything you've told me of life,
   I won't forget a word of it.

PSALM 119:9-16

LOVE NEVER LOOKS BACK

I suppose there may be
a hundred different ways
of being in love.

EMMA, CHAPTER 6

LOVE NEVER LOOKS BACK

Love never gives up.
Love cares more for others than for self.
Love doesn't want what it doesn't have.

Love doesn't strut.
Doesn't have a swelled head.
Doesn't force itself on others.

Isn't always "me first."
Doesn't fly off the handle.
Doesn't keep score of the sins of others.
Doesn't revel when others grovel.

Takes pleasure in the flowering of truth.
Puts up with anything
Trusts God always.
Always looks for the best.

Never looks back.
Keeps going to the end.

I CORINTHIANS 13:4-7

OUR INCOMPLETES WILL BE CANCELLED

"There is no charm equal to tenderness of heart," said Emma afterwards to herself. "There is nothing to be compared to it. Warmth and tenderness of heart, with an affectionate, open manner, will beat all the clearness of head in the world, for attraction. I am sure it will. It is tenderness of heart which I have it not, but makes my dear father so generally beloved which gives Isabella all her popularity. I know how to prize and respect it. Harriet is my superior in all the charm and all the felicity it gives. Dear Harriet! I would not change you for the clearest-headed, longest-sighted, best-judging female breathing."

EMMA, CHAPTER 31

OUR INCOMPLETES WILL BE CANCELLED

Love never dies.
Inspired speech will be over some day.
Praying in tongues will end.
Understanding will reach its limit.

We know only a portion of the truth,
and what we say about God is always incomplete.
But when the Complete arrives,
our incompletes will be canceled.

I CORINTHIANS 13:8-10

LEAVE YOUR SECLUSION

Ah! there is nothing like staying at home, for real comfort. Nobody can be more devoted to home than I am. I was quite a proverb for it at Maple Grove. Many a time has Selina said, when she has been going to Bristol, "I really cannot get this girl to move from the house. I absolutely must go in by myself, though I hate being stuck up in the barouche-landau without a companion; but Augusta, I believe, with her own good will, would never stir beyond the park paling." Many a time she has said so; and yet I am no advocate for entire seclusion.

EMMA, CHAPTER 32

LEAVE YOUR SECLUSION

Get up, my dear friend,
    fair and beautiful lover—come to me!
Look around you: Winter is over;
    the winter rains are over, gone!
Spring flowers are in blossom all over.
    The whole world's a choir—and singing!
Spring warblers are filling the forest
    with sweet arpeggios.
Lilacs are exuberantly purple and perfumed,
    and cherry trees fragrant with blossoms.
Oh, get up, dear friend,
    my fair and beautiful lover—come to me!
Come, my shy and modest dove—
    leave your seclusion, come out in the open.
Let me see your face,
    let me hear your voice.
For your voice is soothing
    and your face is ravishing.

SONG OF SONGS 2:10-14

75

SET YOUR INSTRUCTIONS TO MUSIC

"I absolutely cannot do without music. It is a necessary of life to me; and having always been used to a very musical society, both at Maple Grove and in Bath, it would have been a most serious sacrifice.... 'But,' said I, 'to be quite honest, I do not think I can live without something of a musical society. I condition for nothing else; but without music, life would be a blank for me.'"

EMMA, CHAPTER 32

SET YOUR INSTRUCTIONS TO MUSIC

Remember what you said to me, your servant—
*   I hang on to these words for dear life!*
These words hold me up in bad times;
*   yes, your promises rejuvenate me.*
The insolent ridicule me without mercy,
*   but I don't budge from your revelation.*
I watch for your ancient landmark words,
*   and know I'm on the right track.*
But when I see the wicked ignore your directions,
*   I'm beside myself with anger.*
I set your instructions to music
*   and sing them as I walk this pilgrim way.*

PSALM 119:49-54

WE HAVE TO CELEBRATE

Such schemes as these are nothing without numbers. One cannot have too large a party. A large party secures its own amusement. And she is a good-natured woman after all. One could not leave her out.

EMMA, CHAPTER 42

WE HAVE TO CELEBRATE

Jesus said, "All this time his older son was out in the field. When the day's work was done he came in. As he approached the house, he heard the music and dancing. Calling over one of the houseboys, he asked what was going on. He told him, 'Your brother came home. Your father has ordered a feast—barbecued beef!—because he has him home safe and sound.'

"The older brother stalked off in an angry sulk and refused to join in. His father came out and tried to talk to him, but he wouldn't listen. The son said, 'Look how many years I've stayed here serving you, never giving you one moment of grief, but have you ever thrown a party for me and my friends? Then this son of yours who has thrown away your money on whores shows up and you go all out with a feast!'

"His father said, 'Son, you don't understand. You're with me all the time, and everything that is mine is yours—but this is a wonderful time, and we had to celebrate. This brother of yours was dead, and he's alive! He was lost, and he's found!'"

LUKE 15:25-32

WORDS CAN BE YOUR DAMNATION

"The best fruit in England—everybody's favorite—always wholesome. These the finest beds and finest sorts. —Delightful to gather for one's self—the only way of really enjoying them. Morning decidedly the best time—never tired—every sort good—hautboy infinitely superior—no comparison—the others hardly eatable—hautboys very scarce—Chili preferred—white wood finest flavor of all—price of strawberries in London—abundance about Bristol—Maple Grove—cultivation—beds when to be renewed—gardeners thinking exactly different—no general rule—gardeners never to be put out of their way—delicious fruit—only too rich to be eaten much of—inferior to cherries—currants more refreshing—only objection to gathering strawberries the stooping—glaring sun—tired to death—could bear it no longer—must go and sit in the shade."

EMMA, CHAPTER 42

WORDS CAN BE YOUR DAMNATION

Jesus said, "If you grow a healthy tree, you'll pick healthy fruit. If you grow a diseased tree, you'll pick worm-eaten fruit. The fruit tells you about the tree.

"You have minds like a snake pit! How do you suppose what you say is worth anything when you are so foul-minded? It's your heart, not the dictionary, that gives meaning to your words. A good person produces good deeds and words season after season. An evil person is a blight on the orchard. Let me tell you something: Every one of these careless words is going to come back to haunt you. There will be a time of Reckoning. Words are powerful; take them seriously. Words can be your salvation. Words can also be your damnation."

MATTHEW 12:33-37

YOU'VE CAPTURED MY HEART

Seldom, very seldom, does complete truth belong to any human disclosure; seldom can it happen that something is not a little disguised, or a little mistaken; but where, as in this case, though the conduct is mistaken, the feelings are not, it may not be very material. Mr. Knightley could not impute to Emma a more relenting heart than she possessed, or a heart more disposed to accept of his.

EMMA, CHAPTER 49

YOU'VE CAPTURED MY HEART

You've captured my heart, dear friend.
 You looked at me, and I fell in love.
 One look my way and I was hopelessly in love!
How beautiful your love, dear, dear friend—
 far more pleasing than a fine, rare wine,
 your fragrance more exotic than select spices.
The kisses of your lips are honey, my love,
 every syllable you speak a delicacy to savor.
Your clothes smell like the wild outdoors,
 the ozone scent of high mountains.
Dear lover and friend, you're a secret garden,
 a private and pure fountain.

SONG OF SONGS 4:9-12

83

BE ALERT

"If I loved you less, I might be able to talk about it more. But you know what I am. You hear nothing but truth from me. I have blamed you, and lectured you, and you have borne it as no other woman in England would have borne it. Bear with the truths I would tell you now, dearest Emma, as well as you have borne with them. The manner, perhaps, may have as little to recommend them. God knows, I have been a very indifferent lover. But you understand me. Yes, you see, you understand my feelings—and will return them if you can. At present, I ask only to hear, once to hear your voice."

EMMA, CHAPTER 49

BE ALERT

Jesus said:
"Be alert.
If you see your friend going wrong, correct him.
If he responds, forgive him.
Even if it's personal against you
and repeated seven times through the day,
and seven times he says, 'I'm sorry, I won't do it again,'
forgive him."

LUKE 17:3-4

YOU'RE SO STEADY

The whole being explained, many obliging things were said by the Miss Thorpes of their wish of being better acquainted with her; of being considered as already friends, through the friendship of their brothers, etc., which Catherine heard with pleasure, and answered with all the pretty expressions she could command; and, as the first proof of amity, she was soon invited to accept an arm of the eldest Miss Thorpe, and take a turn with her about the room. Catherine was delighted with this extension of her Bath acquaintance, and almost forgot Mr. Tilney while she talked to Miss Thorpe. Friendship is certainly the finest balm for the pangs of disappointed love.

NORTHANGER ABBEY, CHAPTER 4

YOU'RE SO STEADY

You need to know, friends,
that thanking God over and over for you
is not only a pleasure;
it's a must. We have to do it.
Your faith is growing phenomenally;
your love for each other is developing wonderfully.
Why, it's only right that we give thanks.
We're so proud of you;
you're so steady and determined in your faith
despite all the hard times that have come down on you.

2 THESSALONIANS 1:3-4

DOWN TO THE LAST DETAIL

"Oh! It is only a novel!" replies the young lady, while she lays down her book with affected indifference, or momentary shame. "It is only Cecilia, or Camilla, or Belinda"; or, in short, only some work in which the greatest powers of the mind are displayed, in which the most thorough knowledge of human nature, the happiest delineation of its varieties, the liveliest effusions of wit and humor, are conveyed to the world in the best-chosen language.

NORTHANGER ABBEY, CHAPTER 5

DOWN TO THE LAST DETAIL

Heaven and Earth were finished,
  down to the last detail.
By the seventh day
  God had finished his work.
On the seventh day
  he rested from all his work.
God blessed the seventh day.
  He made it a Holy Day
Because on that day he rested from his work,
  all the creating God had done.
This is the story of how it all started,
  of Heaven and Earth when they were created.

GENESIS 2:1-4

KNOWING THE SCORE

"Scold them! Do you scold them for not admiring her?"

"Yes, that I do. There is nothing I would not do for those who are really my friends. I have no notion of loving people by halves; it is not my nature. My attachments are always excessively strong. I told Captain Hunt at one of our assemblies this winter that if he was to tease me all night, I would not dance with him, unless he would allow Miss Andrews to be as beautiful as an angel. The men think us incapable of real friendship, you know, and I am determined to show them the difference. Now, if I were to hear anybody speak slightingly of you, I should fire up in a moment…."

NORTHANGER ABBEY, CHAPTER 6

KNOWING THE SCORE

Hardheaded, harder than rock,
*   they wouldn't change.*
Then I said to myself, "Well, these are just poor people.
*   They don't know any better.*
They were never taught anything about GOD.
*   They never went to prayer meetings.*
I'll find some people from the best families.
*   I'll talk to them.*
They'll know what's going on, the way GOD works.
*   They'll know the score."*
But they were no better! Rebels all!
*   Off doing their own thing.*

JEREMIAH 5:3-5

JOY IN THE NOW

This was a pitch of friendship beyond Catherine.

"You are so like your dear brother," continued Isabella, "that I quite doted on you the first moment I saw you. But so it always is with me; the first moment settles everything. The very first day that Morland came to us last Christmas—the very first moment I beheld him—my heart was irrecoverably gone."

NORTHANGER ABBEY, CHAPTER 15

JOY IN THE NOW

After looking at the way things are on this earth,
here's what I've decided is the best way to live:
Take care of yourself, have a good time,
and make the most of whatever job you have
for as long as God gives you life.
And that's about it.
That's the human lot....
God deals out joy in the present, the now.
It's useless to brood....

ECCLESIASTES 5:18-20

NEVER PATRONIZING, NEVER CONDESCENDING

"But now you love a hyacinth. So much the better. You have gained a new source of enjoyment, and it is well to have as many holds upon happiness as possible. Besides, a taste for flowers is always desirable in your sex, as a means of getting you out of doors, and tempting you to more frequent exercise than you would otherwise take. And though the love of a hyacinth may be rather domestic, who can tell, the sentiment once raised, but you may in time come to love a rose?"

"But I do not want any such pursuit to get me out of doors. The pleasure of walking and breathing fresh air is enough for me, and in fine weather I am out more than half my time. Mamma says I am never within."

"At any rate, however, I am pleased that you have learnt to love a hyacinth. The mere habit of learning to love is the thing; and a teachableness of disposition in a young lady is a great blessing."

NORTHANGER ABBEY, CHAPTER 22

NEVER PATRONIZING, NEVER CONDESCENDING

Even though we had some standing as Christ's apostles,
we never threw our weight around
or tried to come across as important,
with you or anyone else.
We weren't aloof with you.
We took you just as you were.
We were never patronizing,
never condescending,
but we cared for you the way a mother cares for her children.
We loved you dearly.
Not content to just pass on the Message,
we wanted to give you our hearts.
And we did.

I THESSALONIANS 2:6-8

FREE TO LIVE A FREE LIFE

The happiness with which their time now passed, every employment voluntary, every laugh indulged, every meal a scene of ease and good humor, walking where they liked and when they liked, their hours, pleasures, and fatigues at their own command, made her thoroughly sensible of the restraint which the general's presence had imposed, and most thankfully feel their present release from it. Such ease and such delights made her love the place and the people more and more every day.

NORTHANGER ABBEY, CHAPTER 28

FREE TO LIVE A FREE LIFE

Christ has set us free to live a free life.
So take your stand!
Never again let anyone put a harness of slavery on you.

GALATIANS 5:1

DON'T INDULGE YOUR EGO

How quick come the reasons
for approving what we like!

PERSUASION, CHAPTER 2

DON'T INDULGE YOUR EGO

*Don't indulge your ego
at the expense of your soul.*

I PETER 2:11

SMOOTH SAILING

"But I hate to hear you talking so like a fine gentleman, and as if women were all fine ladies, instead of rational creatures. We none of us expect to be in smooth water all our days."

PERSUASION, CHAPTER 8

SMOOTH SAILING

One day Jesus and his disciples got in a boat. "Let's cross the lake," he said. And off they went. It was smooth sailing, and he fell asleep. A terrific storm came up suddenly on the lake. Water poured in, and they were about to capsize. They woke Jesus: "Master, Master, we're going to drown!"

Getting to his feet, he told the wind, "Silence!" and the waves, "Quiet down!" They did it. The lake became smooth as glass.

LUKE 8:22-24

BE GLAD IN YOUR GOD

Her pleasure in the walk must arise from the exercise and the day, from the view of the last smiles of the year upon the tawny leaves and withered hedges, and from repeating to herself some few of the thousand poetical descriptions extant of autumn, that season of peculiar and inexhaustible influence on the mind of taste and tenderness, that season which has drawn from every poet, worthy of being read, some attempt at description, or some lines of feeling.

PERSUASION, CHAPTER 10

BE GLAD IN YOUR GOD

Children of Zion, celebrate!
*   Be glad in your GOD.*
He's giving you a teacher
*   to train you how to live right—*
Teaching, like rain out of heaven, showers of words
*   to refresh and nourish your soul, just as he used to do.*
And plenty of food for your body—silos full of grain,
*   casks of wine and barrels of olive oil.*

JOEL 2:23-24

103

SEND ME!

Yet, in spite of all this, Anne had reason to believe that she had moments only of languor and depression, to hours of occupation and enjoyment. How could it be? She watched, observed, reflected, and finally determined that this was not a case of fortitude or of resignation only. A submissive spirit might be patient, a strong understanding would supply resolution, but here was something more; here was that elasticity of mind, that disposition to be comforted, that power of turning readily from evil to good, and of finding employment which carried her out of herself, which was from nature alone. It was the choicest gift of Heaven; and Anne viewed her friend as one of those instances in which, by a merciful appointment, it seems designed to counterbalance almost every other want.

PERSUASION, CHAPTER 17

SEND ME!

Then one of the angel-seraphs flew to me. He held a live coal that he had taken with tongs from the altar. He touched my mouth with the coal and said:

"Look. This coal has touched your lips.
 Gone your guilt,
 your sins wiped out."
And then I heard the voice of the Master:
 "Whom shall I send?
 Who will go for us?"
I spoke up,
 "I'll go.
 Send me!"

ISAIAH 6:6-8

LOYAL COMMITMENTS

I can listen no longer in silence. I must speak to you by such means as are within my reach. You pierce my soul. I am half agony, half hope. Tell me not that I am too late, that such precious feelings are gone forever. I offer myself to you again with a heart even more your own than when you almost broke it, eight years and a half ago. Dare not say that man forgets sooner than woman, that his love has an earlier death. I have loved none but you. Unjust I may have been, weak and resentful I have been, but never inconstant.

PERSUASION, CHAPTER 23

LOYAL COMMITMENTS

But what happens when we live God's way?
He brings gifts into our lives,
much the same way that fruit appears in an orchard
—things like affection for others,
exuberance about life,
serenity.
We develop a willingness to stick with things,
a sense of compassion in the heart,
and a conviction that a basic holiness
permeates things and people.
We find ourselves involved in loyal commitments,
not needing to force our way in life,
able to marshal and direct our energies wisely.

GALATIANS 5:22-23

MEDITATE DAY AND NIGHT

At last Anne was at home again, and happier than any one in that house could have conceived. All the surprise and suspense, and every other painful part of the morning dissipated by this conversation, she re-entered the house so happy as to be obliged to find an alloy in some momentary apprehensions of its being impossible to last. An interval of meditation, serious and grateful, was the best corrective of everything dangerous in such high-wrought felicity; and she went to her room, and grew steadfast and fearless in the thankfulness of her enjoyment.

PERSUASION, CHAPTER 23

MEDITATE DAY AND NIGHT

GOD *said to Joshua: "Give it everything you have, heart and soul. Make sure you carry out The Revelation that Moses commanded you, every bit of it. Don't get off track, either left or right, so as to make sure you get to where you're going. And don't for a minute let this Book of The Revelation be out of mind. Ponder and meditate on it day and night, making sure you practice everything written in it. Then you'll get where you're going; then you'll succeed. Haven't I commanded you? Strength! Courage! Don't be timid; don't get discouraged. GOD, your God, is with you every step you take."*

JOSHUA 1:6-9

YOUR LIFE COUNTS FOR PLENTY

May we now, and on each return of night, consider how the past day has been spent by us, what have been our prevailing thoughts, words, and actions during it, and how far we can acquit ourselves of evil.

MINOR WORKS

YOUR LIFE COUNTS FOR PLENTY

Now Jesus turned to address his disciples, along with the crowd that had gathered with them. "The religion scholars and Pharisees are competent teachers in God's Law. You won't go wrong in following their teachings on Moses. But be careful about following them. They talk a good line, but they don't live it. They don't take it into their hearts and live it out in their behavior. It's all spit-and-polish veneer....

"Don't let people do that to you, put you on a pedestal like that. You all have a single Teacher, and you are all classmates. Don't set people up as experts over your life, letting them tell you what to do. Save that authority for God; let him tell you what to do. No one else should carry the title of 'Father'; you have only one Father, and he's in heaven. And don't let people maneuver you into taking charge of them. There is only one Life-Leader for you and them—Christ.

"Do you want to stand out? Then step down. Be a servant. If you puff yourself up, you'll get the wind knocked out of you. But if you're content to simply be yourself, your life will count for plenty."

MATTHEW 23:1-3, 8-12

111

WHAT GOD DOES AND WHAT YOU DO

Give us grace, almighty father, so to pray, as to deserve to be heard, to address you with our hearts, as with our lips. You are everywhere present, from you no secret can be hid. May the knowledge of this, teach us to fix our thoughts on you, with reverence and devotion that we pray not in vain.

MINOR WORKS

WHAT GOD DOES AND WHAT YOU DO

Jesus said, "In prayer there is a connection between what God does and what you do. You can't get forgiveness from God, for instance, without also forgiving others. If you refuse to do your part, you cut yourself off from God's part.

"When you practice some appetite-denying discipline to better concentrate on God, don't make a production out of it. It might turn you into a small-time celebrity but it won't make you a saint. If you 'go into training' inwardly, act normal outwardly. Shampoo and comb your hair, brush your teeth, wash your face. God doesn't require attention-getting devices. He won't overlook what you are doing; he'll reward you well."

MATTHEW 6:14-15

SET THE WORLD RIGHT

Teach us Almighty Father, to consider this solemn truth, as we should do, that we may feel the importance of every day, and every hour as it passes, and earnestly strive to make a better use of what your goodness may yet bestow on us, than we have done of the time past. Give us grace to endeavour after a truly Christian spirit to seek to attain that temper of forbearance and patience of which our blessed savior has set us the highest example; and which, while it prepares us for the spiritual happiness of the life to come, will secure to us the best enjoyment of what this world can give.

MINOR WORKS

SET THE WORLD RIGHT

Jesus said, "The world is full of so-called prayer warriors who are prayer-ignorant. They're full of formulas and programs and advice, peddling techniques for getting what you want from God. Don't fall for that nonsense. This is your Father you are dealing with, and he knows better than you what you need. With a God like this loving you, you can pray very simply. Like this:

Our Father in heaven,
Reveal who you are.
Set the world right;
Do what's best—
     as above, so below.
Keep us alive with three square meals.
Keep us forgiven with you and forgiving others.
Keep us safe from ourselves and the Devil.
You're in charge!
You can do anything you want!
You're ablaze in beauty!
     Yes. Yes. Yes.

MATTHEW 6:7-13

Rachel Hart Winter brings a wealth of experience in scholarly research, higher education administration and teaching, and pastoral ministry to her work as director of St. Catherine of Siena Center at Dominican University, River Forest, Illinois. She also serves as adjunct professor at Dominican University, where she teaches classes on biomedical and healthcare ethics. Her academic credits include a BA in Behavioral Neuroscience from Lehigh University, and a Master of Theological Studies and a PhD from Loyola University Chicago. Her theological interests lie at the intersection of ecology and theology, drawing from the Bible, Catholic social teaching, ecotheology, and feminist theory. She is a co-author of *Healing Earth* through the International Jesuit Ecology Project and has written various articles and chapters for publication. She is married to Patrick Winter and has three children: Joseph, Thomas, and Catherine. She loves to read and has always enjoyed using literature, poetry, and music as creative entry points to prayer and meditation.

LITERARY PORTALS TO PRAYER™

Louisa May Alcott*

Hans Christian Andersen*

Jane Austen

Charles Dickens*

Elizabeth Gaskell*

Herman Melville*

William Shakespeare*

Edith Wharton

Walt Whitman

*An enhanced-size edition available for each of these titles.

800-397-2282 • ACTAPUBLICATIONS.COM